LISTENER

CLASSICAL
mood

Serenity

Serenity

*L*ife today hurtles along at such a punishing pace that most individuals could benefit from a calming influence. Allow this volume of *In Classical Mood* to provide that much-needed serenity. Let the wistful melodies of some of the greatest composers—including Beethoven's *The Emperor*, Schubert's *An die Musik*, and Pachelbel's *Canon in D Major*—help you drift into a relaxing world of your own. This is music with a gentle, soothing sound to help restore peace in your life and surround yourself in an air of contentment.

THE LISTENER'S GUIDE — WHAT THE SYMBOLS MEAN

THE COMPOSERS
Their lives... their loves..
their legacies...

THE MUSIC
Explanation... analysis...
interpretation...

THE INSPIRATION
How works of genius
came to be written

THE BACKGROUND
People, places, and events
linked to the music

© MCMXCVI IMP AB   In Classical Mood™   IMP AB, produced under license by IMP Inc.   Printed in China.   US P 2201 12 011

Contents

FELIX MENDELSSOHN *1809–1847*

Violin Concerto in E Minor,

OPUS 64: SECOND MOVEMENT

No instrument can compete with the violin's ability to carry a melody so serenely, as Felix Mendelssohn demonstrates here with this lovely opening tune. The original melody returns after the middle section of the movement, before finally drifting away under the softest of chords on flutes and clarinets.

KEY CONCERTO

Mendelssohn's *Violin Concerto* is a key work in the history of concerto writing, breaking new ground in at least two important ways. In the first movement, for example, the violin enters with the main theme almost at once, without the traditional orchestral introduction. The other development is that the concerto's three movements are played without a break. Beethoven had already adopted the practice of linking movements together in some of his concertos, and Mendelssohn took the process still further.

A PARTICULAR SOLOIST

Many concertos have been written with a particular soloist in mind. In this case it was the German violinist Ferdinand David *(right, inset)*. He was an orchestra leader at the famous Leipzig concert hall, the Gewandhaus *(right)*, where Mendelssohn himself conducted. Mendelssohn sought David's advice on every technical aspect of this concerto, and David gave its first performance, in Leipzig in 1845.

SWAN SONG

This serene violin concerto which Mendelssohn *(left)* wrote three years before his death turned out to be his last major orchestral work. Ill health, brought about mainly by exhaustion from overwork coupled with his grief over his sister's death, took its toll and he died at the age of just thirty-eight.

K E Y   N O T E S

The middle part of the slow movement contains some examples of double stopping in the solo part. This entails playing two notes at once, which adds great richness to the melodic line.

ANTONIO VIVALDI *1678–1741*

Guitar Concerto in D Major

SECOND MOVEMENT

The sound of the guitar in this movement enters with a gentle strumming effect and lulls the listener into a state of repose. Its solo line traces a gentle melody above a soft and silken background of sound from the accompanying strings. This is music of untroubled peace.

FOR THE LUTE

Antonio Vivaldi originally wrote this guitar concerto as a piece for the lute—another plucked string instrument—with an accompaniment of two violins and a double bass. But composers of the Baroque period, such as Vivaldi himself, Bach, and Handel, knew how to get the maximum potential out of any piece of music, adapting and rearranging their compositions to suit any occasion and instrument.

VIRTUOSO GUITARISTS

This century has seen a rise in the number of great virtuosos. Among them is John Williams *(right)* who, as well as performing all the great guitar concertos, has also enjoyed success with his classical interpretations of modern pop music.

CHAMPIONING THE GUITAR

Quiet and unassertive, the guitar has never held center stage in the concert hall, but it has had its champions. In addition to Vivaldi, Boccherini and Spanish composer Fernando Sor both wrote many works for the instrument. In this century, Joaquin Rodrigo, William Walton, and André Previn have also written for it. The great virtuoso violinist Niccolò Paganini *(left)* loved the guitar, too. He temporarily gave up performing the violin and taught himself the guitar, writing several charming pieces for the instrument.

KEY NOTES

The modern Spanish or classical guitar has six strings, tuned to the notes E, A, D, G, B, and E in ascending order of pitch. Different tunings are sometimes adopted by different players for particular works.

LUIGI BOCCHERINI
1743–1805

String Quintet in E Major

NO.5, OPUS 13

Commonly referred to as the *Minuet*—after the most popular of all dances throughout the old royal courts and palaces of Europe in the 17th century—this arrangement for string orchestra was Luigi Boccherini's most important work. As the main tune comes tripping lightly in on the violins, the listener can imagine the dancers taking the small, dainty steps that are characteristic of the minuet. A brief middle section then enters, moving gracefully up and down the scale in a timeless fashion.

A PROLIFIC COMPOSER

The Italian composer Luigi Boccherini *(right)* was once a famous name in classical music. A contemporary of Haydn and Mozart, he was a prolific composer of chamber music and wrote 154 string quintets and 91 string quartets, as well as 30 symphonies and 11 concertos. He was also a highly accomplished cellist and was much in demand, both as a composer and a performer. It certainly is sad that the *Minuet* is the only piece for which he is widely remembered today from his whole vast output of music.

SPANISH CONNECTION

Boccherini spent many years in Spain. He had already achieved great success as a composer and cello player in Paris and is thought to have gone to Madrid *(right)* on the recommendation of the Spanish ambassador in Paris. He certainly made a good impression when he got there, becoming a highly paid musician to the Spanish court. Even the ups and downs of the Napoleonic Wars worked

in his favor when Napoleon's brother Lucien, who was French ambassador to Madrid, called upon Boccherini's services. The house in which he lived in Madrid still stands today and bears a plaque commemorating the composer's residency. But after 1787, he no longer had a patron and fell on harder times, dying in poverty at age sixty-two in a single room in Madrid.

ON FILM

Boccherini's minuet reached an even wider audience in the 1950s when it was used in the classic Ealing Studios comedy-thriller *The Lady Killers*. The film centered around a group of bungling London crooks who, to cover up their plotting, pretended to be rehearsing this piece—in actual fact they simply played a gramophone record. The film starred *(clockwise from bottom left)* Alec Guinness, Herbert Lom, Peter Sellers, Cecil Parker, Danny Green, and Katie Johnson.

MUSICAL PATRONS

The huge number of works composed by Boccherini *(below)*, particularly in the 1770s, can be partly explained by the era in which he lived. The 18th-century was a period where thousands of works for stringed instruments were commissioned by music-loving aristocratic patrons who enjoyed playing them after dinner. Among Boccherini's many benefactors were the Prussian king Friedrich Wilhelm II and the Spanish Infante Don Luis. Don Luis's elder brother, King Charles III of Spain, even paid Boccherini a small pension.

KEY NOTES

The Tuscan town of Lucca was the birthplace of two of Italy's most famous composers— Luigi Boccherini in 1743 and Giacomo Puccini some 115 years later in 1858.

FRÉDÉRIC CHOPIN
1810-1849

Andante Spianato in G

OPUS 22

The spirit and style of this charming music is very much in the mood of Frédérick Chopin's better-known solo piano *Nocturnes*. A clear, calm melody unfolds above a gently flowing left-handed accompaniment. A second pensive snatch of melody is, perhaps, even more haunting than the opening and adds a finishing touch to the dreamlike effect of the work.

IN CONCERT

Chopin wrote a *Grande Polonaise Brillante* for piano and orchestra as a showpiece for himself to perform at concerts. He later added the solo piano piece *Andante Spianato* as an introduction to the work. Both parts are still played today, both together and as independent pieces of music.

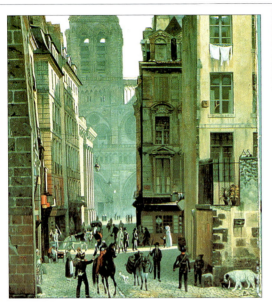

CHOPIN AND LISZT

Chopin and Liszt, the two greatest pianist-composers of their age, met in Paris *(above)*. Liszt helped the young man from Poland settle in the French capital and even introduced him to the female novelist George Sand, who was to become the great love of Chopin's life. But the two men had very different personalities. Chopin, fastidious, aloof, and a very private person, found Liszt's showy style rather embarrassing and even vulgar.

INSPIRATION

Spanish composer and pianist Enrique Granados (1867–1916) was particularly taken with Frédéric Chopin's *Andante Spianato*. Granados *(below)* admired the piece so much that it became the inspiration for the epilogue, or concluding part, to his own *Escenas Romanticas* for the piano.

KEY NOTES

The Italian word spianato *literally means "smoothed out." So* Andante Spianato *means a soft and gentle piece, taken at a leisurely pace.*

SIR EDWARD ELGAR *1857–1934*

Serenade for Strings in E Minor

OPUS 20: ALLEGRETTO

In this, the third movement from one of Sir Edward Elgar's favorite compositions, the opening melody rises lightly and elegantly up the scale. A brief new melody enters toward the end of the piece, capturing the serenity of a beautiful summer morning.

EVENING SERENADE

Back in the 18th century, serenades were originally composed as music to be performed in the evening. But with the passing of time, the title of serenade has taken on a broader meaning. Today it often describes a generally relaxed and genial composition, with no particular time of day or night in mind.

KEY NOTES

Allegretto *means "little allegro." In other words, fast and lively but a little more restrained in pace and mood than a bright and breezy allegro.*

FRANZ SCHUBERT *1797–1828*

An die Musik

D547

ranz Schubert composed *An die Musik* in 1817 and the charming song has been immortalized ever since. The soothing piano accompaniment follows the quietly ecstatic vocal melody as though it were a second voice. There are few pieces as adept as this one at raising the listener's spirits.

THE WORDS OF THE SONG

The words of this famous song, or *Lied* as it is called in German, were written by the composer's good friend, the poet Franz von Schober. Few of us would know his work today, were it not for Schubert's use of his verses.

KEY NOTES

Two of Schubert's other songs from 1817 are Der Tod und das Mädchen *(Death and the Maiden)* and Die Forelle *(The Trout).*

CAMILLE SAINT-SAËNS *1835–1921*

The Carnival of the Animals

THE AQUARIUM

Rippling runs and *arpeggios* (chords where notes are played one after the other) on the piano conjure up an aquatic scene in this "musical" aquarium. The sinuous melody of the violins and flute suggests fishes gliding through the water, while the subtle variations in the piece all help to paint a magical picture of underwater life.

WATER THERAPY

 It is widely believed that images and sounds of water, such as a an ocean *(right)*, running stream, gentle waterfall, or even a refreshing fountain, have a calming effect on people. Many doctors' and dentists' waiting rooms have aquariums to calm the nerves of apprehensive patients.

WIDE INTERESTS

Camille Saint-Saëns was a man of wide interests who had a lively curiosity in many other subjects besides music. He was an avid and enthusiastic historian, with a special knowledge of ancient Roman art and architecture. He learned Latin under a private tutor, and it was a matter of great regret to him that he never studied Greek. Astronomy was another keen interest of his. He once even broke off an important rehearsal in order to watch an eclipse of the sun.

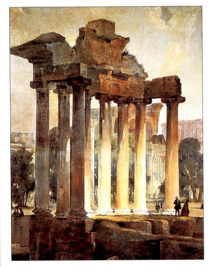

Camille Saint-Saëns was a great authority on the history and architecture of ancient Rome, including Naples, Pompeii, and the Roman forum (left).

A LONG CAREER

The French composer Camille Saint-Saëns *(right)* enjoyed an extremely long and successful career. A child prodigy, giving his first piano recital at the age of eleven, he composed operas, symphonies, concertos, symphonic poems, and chamber and piano music with equal ease and assurance. He was also an organist at the fashionable Madeleine church in Paris for many years. Showered with honors, at home and abroad, he died in Algiers in the then-French colony of Algeria at age eighty-six.

WATER MUSIC

Claude Debussy *(below)* may well have been inspired by his compatriot Saint-Saëns's rippling piano composition in *The Aquarium* when he came to write such impressionistic piano pieces as "Reflets dans l'eau" ("Reflections in the water") and "Poissons d'or" ("Goldfish"), from *Images*, Set 1 and 2.

KEY NOTES

Throughout his long life, Saint-Saëns had an incurable wanderlust. North America, South America, and Sri Lanka were some of the places he visited before spending his last years in Algiers.

EDVARD GRIEG *1843–1907*

Elegiac Melody

NO.2, OPUS 34, "THE LAST SPRING"

*S*o much of Edvard Grieg's music is written for string orchestra, with its rich but soft and expressive tone. Here, the strings carry the lovely heartfelt melody to a high point of emotion before allowing it to slowly fade away. The melody is reminiscent of the brief but intense springtime in Norway, Grieg's homeland.

DEATH IN SPRING

This piece is one of *Two Elegiac Melodies*—arrangements for string orchestra of two of Grieg's finest songs. The song on which this one is based is called "The Last Spring." It concerns a dying poet enjoying spring for the very last time and touchingly blends the mix of joy and sadness that he experiences during his final days.

KEY NOTES

An elegiac originally denoted a poem or song written as a lament for the dead. The title has now broadened its meaning somewhat, but it still carries a message of sad farewells.

FREDERICK DELIUS *1862–1934*

Florida Suite

AT NIGHT

A solo oboe enters gently, followed by other woodwind instruments. There is a soft, romantic call on the horns, then the strings make their entry with a melody suggestive of the setting sun. Toward the end, the beckoning horns are heard again, welcoming nightfall. It evokes the kind of warm, scented night that Frederick Delius must have loved during the years he spent in Florida—a time when Florida was still a haven of untouched natural beauty.

BACK FROM HIS TRAVELS

The *Florida Suite* was written after Delius had returned from Florida, where he had been managing an orange grove, and enrolled at Leipzig Conservatory for further musical studies. *Florida Suite* was first performed in Leipzig in 1888, and because it was not performed again for over fifty years, this was the only occasion Delius ever heard this work in his lifetime.

KEY NOTES

One of his most well-known pieces, Delius's Florida Suite is made up of four haunting movements. The other three are entitled: "Daybreak," "By the River," and "Sunset."

JOHANN PACHELBEL *1653–1706*

Canon in D Major

*J*ohann Pachelbel opens this canon with a simple phrase in the bass or "continuo" part, which is repeated over and over again, while the violins proceed to weave the melodic line of the canon high above it. Such music conveys a wonderful sense of timelessness. The effect is also quite hypnotic—the perfect musical antidote for all the stresses of modern life.

ROUND AND ROUND

A canon is a type of musical composition, or part of a composition, in which several instruments or voices —while playing or singing the same melody—come in at different stages. By doing so, they overlap each other. Simple forms of a canon are called "catches" or "rounds." "Three Blind Mice" and "Row Your Boat" are particularly well-known examples of this very clever type of musical composition.

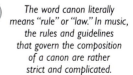

UNDERVALUED

The German composer Johann Pachelbel is remembered by most people today on the strength of just one piece, *Canon in D Major*. But Pachelbel has an important place in musical history. Born in the German city of Nuremberg *(right)*, he was a fine organist and choirmaster. He was also a prolific composer of organ music, pieces for the harpsichord, arias, chamber works, choral motets, and church music. His music had a particularly strong influence on his young contemporary J.S. Bach.

Right: *The lavish title page of* Hexachordum Apollinis, *one of Pachabel's many works.*

CLOSE FRIENDS

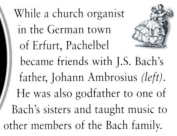

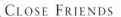

While a church organist in the German town of Erfurt, Pachelbel became friends with J.S. Bach's father, Johann Ambrosius *(left)*. He was also godfather to one of Bach's sisters and taught music to other members of the Bach family.

KEY NOTES

The word canon literally means "rule" or "law." In music, the rules and guidelines that govern the composition of a canon are rather strict and complicated.

LUDWIG VAN BEETHOVEN *1770–1827*

Piano Concerto No.5 in E-flat Major

"THE EMPEROR": SECOND MOVEMENT

It has been said that Beethoven's slow movements are like being stroked by the hand of a giant. In this movement of his final concerto, the strings introduce a calm but noble theme. The piano traces leisurely patterns around it, briefly adds a few pensive notes, settles back into some beautiful trills, then returns to the original theme.

ON THE MOVE

Beethoven was twenty-two when he left Bonn to study in Vienna under Joseph Haydn and Johann Albrechtsberger. For the rest of his life he rarely ventured more than a few miles into the surrounding countryside. But within the city itself he was constantly on the move, from one apartment to the next, in his search for peace and seclusion.

Above: *one of Ludwig van Beethoven's many workrooms in Vienna.*

THE CADENZA

Traditional features of concertos were *cadenzas*—points in the score where the soloist could improvise to show off his own talents. Beethoven followed such a practice until this piece, his last concerto. Instead, he wrote in his own cadenzas to keep strict control over all material in such an important work.

THE MYSTERIOUS EMPEROR

The nickname *The Emperor* attached to this concerto was not assigned by Beethoven. In fact, the story behind the nickname is uncertain. It is thought that Johann Baptist Cramer *(left)*, a German pianist and composer, bestowed it simply to convey the majestic character of the work. One thing for sure is that it does not refer to Napoleon, whom Beethoven came to dislike when he crowned himself "Emperor of the French."

KEY NOTES

Two of Beethoven's other works which have acquired unofficial nicknames are the "Moonlight" and "Tempest" piano sonatas.

CLAUDE DEBUSSY 1862–1918

Petite Suite
EN BATEAU

En Bateau, or "In a Boat," suggests an outing on a river or lake. The leisurely, gently undulating rhythm and dreamy-sounding melody take the listener on a slow boat trip on a sunny, lazy day. With the lap of the water, the easy movement of the oars, and the soothing motion of the boat itself, the music leads the listener serenely across the waters.

VARIOUS VERSIONS

This early piano piece exists in several versions: as originally written, for piano duet (four hands); for solo piano; and, as here, for orchestra. Both Debussy *(left)* and his younger contemporary, Ravel, spent a good deal of time making various transcriptions or arrangements of their own music. And if they didn't get around to doing it, music publishers would often do it themselves!

KEY NOTES

En Bateau *comes from a small group of pieces collectively entitled* Petite Suite *("Little Suite"). The other movements are:* Cortège *("Funeral Procession"),* Menuet *("Minuet"), and* Ballet.

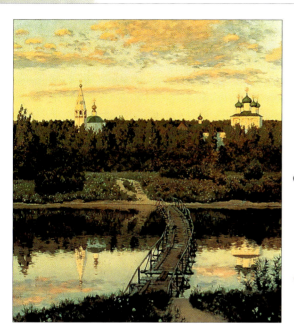

PYOTR TCHAIKOVSKY *1840–1893*

String Quartet No.1 in D

OPUS 11: ANDANTE CANTABILE

This leisurely piece opens with one of the most tender melodies from Pyotr Tchaikovsky's great works. As if that weren't enough, he then gives us a second and equally lovely theme, introduced on the violin to a soft pizzicato accompaniment. The underlying melancholy of the music only enhances its mood of reflection.

FOLK ROOTS

The *String Quartet No.1 in D* dates from the same early period of Tchaikovsky's creative life as the fantasy-overture *Romeo and Juliet*. The quartet's much-loved *Andante Cantabile* movement is based on a folk song which Tchaikovsky first heard on a visit to his sister in the Ukraine in 1869 and it is often performed in an arrangement for string orchestra.

KEY NOTES

The term andante cantabile *is usually used as a directional by composers, meaning "flowing" or "song-like." It is also synonymous with this second movement from Tchaikovsky's string quartet.*

WOLFGANG AMADEUS MOZART
1756–1791

Serenade No.10 in B-flat Major

K361, "GRAN PARTITA":
THIRD MOVEMENT

At a serene and measured pace, thirteen wind instruments embark in perfected agreement upon a stately theme. Then the sound of a single oboe steals in above them with a melody of its own, as clear and pure as a single shaft of sunlight. Wolfgang Amadeus Mozart's movement continues on with the melodic line continually enriched by a pattern of wonderful harmonies. This is a most inspirational piece of music, its mystery and sentiment transporting the listener to a world of almost heavenly peace.

WORK OF GENIUS

Mozart probably began work on this serenade in 1781, around the time he was dismissed from his post with the Archbishop of Salzburg and settled in Vienna, where he tried to make his own way in the world. In the film *Amadeus (right)*, which is a dramatized account of Mozart's life, the composer Salieri proclaims Mozart a genius after hearing this serenade.

OUTDOOR PERFORMANCES

This composition is a superb example of what is called in German, *Harmoniemusik*: music for a band using only wind, brass, and percussion. Such music—which was popular in the 18th century—was often performed outdoors in the open air *(left)*,

because these instruments, compared with strings, carried their sound much further and were easier to carry. A serenade or suite for outdoor use was often called a "cassation," of which Mozart composed several.

KEY NOTES

Mozart's Serenade in B-flat *is popularly known as* "Gran Partita." Gran *means* "grand" *while* Partita *is another name for a* "suite," *or a* "succession of movements."

Credits & Acknowledgments

PICTURE CREDITS

Cover /Title and Contents Pages/ IBC: Images Colour LibraryAKG London: 3(b), 7(t), 8(t): (E. Gaertner: Paris) 10(l), 19(tr & bl), 23; (D. van Alsloot: Procession (detail)): 25(b); E. Lessing: 6, (C. Monet: Boat at Giverny): 22(tr); Bridgeman Art Library, London/Christie's Images (V. Reggianini: A Musical Interlude); Mary Evans Picture Library: 7(b), 10(r); Fine Art Photographic Library/Haynes Fine Art (A.D. Lucas: A Secret Path): 11; Anthony Mitchell Paintings, Nottingham (A.

Beyschlag: At the Piano): 12; Ronald Grant Archive: 8(b), 25(t); Robert Harding Picture Library: 17(t); The Image Bank: 3(br); Images Colour Library: 16; Charles Walker Collection: 24; Lebrecht Collection: 3(tr), 5(b), 9(b), 15(r & l), 19(cr), 21(t & b), 22(bl); B. Morris: 3(t); N. Luckhurst: 5(t); Elizabeth Whiting Associates: 9(t); Neil Lorimer: 20; Larry Prosor/Super Stock: 14(t); Zeta:14(b); Corneel Voigt: 13; Kalt: 18.

All illustrations and symbols: John See